MW00711361

To:

_____

From:

_____

Date:

_____

Message:

_____

_____

A soft
PILLOW
for a tired
HEART

Barbara Johnson

christian
art gifts

Today is here

Whatever your hand finds to do,
do it with all your might ...
~ Ecclesiastes 9:10 ~

Dream not too much of
what you'll do tomorrow,
How well you'll work another year;
Tomorrow's chance you
do not need to borrow –
Today is here.

A fresh start

*Consider him who endured such
opposition from sinful men, so that you
will not grow weary and lose heart.*
~ *Hebrews 12:3* ~

If you fail in one place, that
doesn't make you a failure. Sure,
we all fall, but it's how long you stay
down that counts. Get up, begin
again, and you will know the
joy of a fresh start with Jesus.

Only one me

*I praise you because I am fearfully
and wonderfully made; your works
are wonderful, I know that full well.*
~ Psalm 139:14 ~

I celebrate me!
I am worth everything.
I am unique. In the whole
world there is only one me.
There is only one person
with my talents, my experience,
and my gifts.

The now

*If we confess our sins, he is faithful
and just and will forgive us our sins and
purify us from all unrighteousness.*
~ *1 John 1:9* ~

It doesn't matter my age, color,
or whether I was loved as a child or
not. Let all that go. That belongs
to the past. I belong to the now! It
doesn't matter where I have been,
or what mistakes I've made, or
hurts I have had. I am forgiven.
I am accepted. I'm okay. I
am loved in spite of everything.

A fresh day

He who was seated on the throne said, "I am making everything new ... Write this down, for these words are trustworthy and true."
~ Revelation 21:5 ~

Today can be a fresh day,
a new beginning.
This earth suit will be gone
one day, traded in for
a robe of white –
until then I have today to enjoy!

From where we are

*Do not conform any longer to
the pattern of this world, but be
transformed by the renewing of your
mind. Then you will be able to test
and approve what God's will is ...*
~ Romans 12:2 ~

We can't really live our whole lives
over again, but we can make
progress from where we are
right now to where God wants
us to be. The only time it's too late
to change our lives is when we
reach heaven – God's eternal today.

Minutes of gold

[Make] the most of every opportunity ...
but understand what the Lord's will is.
~ Ephesians 5:16-17 ~

Minutes of Gold.
Two or three minutes –
two or three hours,
What do they mean in this life of ours?
A minute may dry a little lad's tears,
An hour sweep aside
the trouble of years.
Minutes of my time may bring to an end
Hopelessness somewhere,
and bring me a friend.
~ Author Unknown ~

A long-term investment

But I trust in you, O LORD ...
My times are in your hands ...
~ Psalm 31:14-15 ~

You can recover and gain confidence
in your children by remembering
that loving your child is a long-term
investment, not a short-term loan.
Love is worth the time it takes to grow,
and growing a child is not a quick process.

God uses our failures

Therefore, if anyone is in Christ,
he is a new creation; the old
has gone, the new has come!
~ 2 Corinthians 5:17 ~

God uses even our failures to
make better people of us. Jesus
saw men, not as they were, but
as they were to become, filled with his
Spirit and dedicated to his work.
There's nothing wrong with failure.
There's plenty wrong with giving up.

God has planned the future

When I called, you
answered me; you made me
bold and stouthearted.
~ Psalm 138:3 ~

God will bring healing, patience,
and comfort when you don't
think you can survive
another day. Don't grieve
over the past; rejoice that God
has already planned the future.

Never too old to learn

*He who heeds discipline shows the
way to life, but whoever ignores
correction leads others astray.*
~ Proverbs 10:17 ~

Most of us are long past the
time of going to school,
studying, and taking tests. Most
of us are even past preparing
our children for school and tests.
But no matter what our ages,
we are never too old to learn.

What I do today

But seek first his kingdom and his
righteousness, and all these
things wil be given to you as well.
~ Matthew 6:33 ~

This is the beginning of a new day.
God has given me this day to use
as I will. I can waste it – or
use it for good, but what I do
today is important, because I am
exchanging a day of my life for it!

The past is over

Brothers, I do not consider myself yet to have taken hold of it. But one thing I do: Forgetting what is behind and straining toward what is ahead ...
~ Philippians 3:13 ~

No matter what has happened in the past, that is over. No matter how much you wish the past had been different, you cannot change what has already happened. Don't mourn over what is done; rejoice that there is still a future!

Reach out

*Do not be anxious about anything, but in
everything, by prayer and petition, with
thanksgiving, present your requests to God.
And the peace of God, which transcends
all understanding, will guard your
hearts and your minds in Christ Jesus.
~ Philippians 4:6-7 ~*

God is present and ready to help you
right where you are. Reach out in a simple
prayer to Jesus and feel Him now take
your hand. With his hand and power
at work in your life, you, too, can have
your tears turned into joy, your night
into day, your pain into gain, your
failures into successes, your
scars into stars, and
your tragedy into triumph.

18

Embrace the future

This day is sacred to our LORD.
Do not grieve, for the joy
of the LORD is your strength.
~ Nehemiah 8:10 ~

How we look at life can determine
where we will find joy in our
exercise of beginning again.
This is what I wish for you: that you
will find joy in sorrow, let go of
the past, and embrace the future
God has given you today,
and work on using today wisely.

God's grace
for tomorrow

*Those who know your name will
trust in you, for you, LORD, have
never forsaken those who seek you.*
~ Psalm 9:10 ~

Life is not over just because
you have experienced a
devastating blow. Begin again
today, and trust God's
forgiveness to take care of yesterday,
and his grace to take care of tomorrow.

No tragedy
lasts forever

Yet he did not waver through unbelief
regarding the promise of God, but
was strengthened in his faith ...
~ Romans 4:20 ~

While life isn't always the way we want
it, no tragedy lasts forever. Recovery and
survival are in reach. We can walk
together, patiently enduring the
sorrow and depression as we grow
up from the valley onto the mountaintop.
Sorrow may flood you repeatedly,
but each time you will
survive, stronger and
happier than before.

21

The final reward

I have fought the good fight, I have
finished the race, I have kept the faith.
~ 2 Timothy 4:7 ~

There are days when I wonder
what is so great about hanging
in there. For what? And then I
remember the final reward:
standing before the Lord and
knowing I have fought a
good fight, have kept the faith,
and have finished the course.

Accept what you have

Give thanks in all circumstances, for this is God's will for you in Christ Jesus.
~ 1 Thessalonians 5:18 ~

Nothing is perfect, nothing
will be exactly right, but we
can enjoy and appreciate what
we have, not what we wish we
had. We need to learn to
accept what God has for us.

Rainbows from tears

Through the wetness of your tears,
your own sorrow will begin to
glisten. You can go from the pits,
where it is black, to beige, and
then to rainbows, which come
from tears in our lives.
Your constant habit of being a
joy collector will be your therapy.

Joy is the presence of God

The LORD is my shepherd, I shall not be in want. He makes me lie down in green pastures, he leads me beside quiet waters, he restores my soul ...
~ Psalm 23:1-3 ~

Joy is not the absence of suffering but the presence of God. We all go through pain and sorrow, but the presence of God, like a warm, comforting blanket, can shield us and protect us, and allow the deep inner joy to surface, even in the most devastating circumstances.

Make this a love month

Remember this: Whoever sows sparingly will also reap sparingly, and whoever sows generously will also reap generously.
~ 2 Corinthians 9:6 ~

Let's concentrate on making
this month a love month. Let's learn
to love life and it will love us back.
What you give is what you get.
Life is like a boomerang – if you
throw it out it will come back to you.

God has a plan

When I was woven together ...
your eyes saw my unformed
body. All the days ordained for
me were written in your book
before one of them came to be.
~ Psalm 139:15-16 ~

I am absolutely convinced that
life does not happen by chance.
God has a plan; God's plan is full
of His love for us; and God's plan will
succeed! When we are in the midst
of pain it is hard to believe that, but I
know it's true, and I've seen it work!

Love your child unconditionally!

Above all, love each other deeply, because love covers over a multitude of sins.
~ 1 Peter 4:8 ~

Don't forget to love your child unconditionally! He or she may pierce your heart with actions which seem to you to be designed especially to hurt you. But your job is not to judge, not to condemn, not to get revenge. Your job as a Christian and a parent is to love that child in the midst of everything!

Give your love away

*"Greater love has no one
than this, that he lay
down his life for his friends."*
~ John 15:13 ~

Life's greatest joy is to give your
love away. As you allow God's
love to flow through you and
you give that love out, God will
use you to touch another
person who needs
to feel the
warmth of that love.

Spendthrifts in love!

Let no debt remain outstanding,
except the continuing debt to love
one another, for he who loves his
fellowman has fulfilled the law.
~ Romans 13:8 ~

It would be great if we could
all be spendthrifts and just buy
anything in sight. But we can be
spendthrifts in love! Love is the
one treasure that is multiplied by
division. It is the one gift that grows
bigger the more you take from it.

Dwell on God's love

Keep yourselves in God's love as you wait for the mercy of our Lord Jesus Christ to bring you to eternal life.
~ Jude verse 21 ~

When you have "down" days
(and we all do), and you feel that
the black pit has you again,
just dwell on God's love.
How rich and full it is!
Let his love keep you
and give you rest. Just
rest in God's love, which
is a shield around
your hurting heart.

The strength to risk love

We love because he first loved us.
~ 1 John 4:19 ~

Don't be afraid to share your love.
Don't be afraid to give your love
to a wayward child. Nothing will
happen to you and your love
that God isn't ultimately in charge of.
He will give you the strength to
risk your love, and the
glue if your heart breaks
and needs mending.

A fragile thing

*Praise be to the God and Father of
our Lord Jesus Christ, the Father of
compassion and the God of all comfort,
who comforts us in all our troubles ...*
~ 2 Corinthians 1:3-4 ~

This heart of mine is such a
fragile thing. Like fine porcelain,
I could set it on a shelf, but I tend
to put it rather in the midst of life.
Thus it has been broken a
million times. Perhaps the glue
with which God mends it is
stronger that the stuff
of which it is made.
~ Author Unknown ~

Warm compassion

Carry each other's burdens,
and in this way you will
fulfill the law of Christ.
~ Galatians 6:2 ~

So many people are lonely today.
Every time you give someone
else a lift, you get a lift. Compassion
is one healing, uplifting gift
that God gives to each of us to
use. Warm compassion can break
the chains that bind
us and transform a
cold, indifferent
world into a warm,
loving one.

People like you and me

Brothers, think of what you were when
you were called. Not many ... were
wise ... influential ... of noble birth.
~ 1 Corinthians 1:26 ~

Who does God use? He uses
people like you and me. Don't
let past failures hinder you.
Failure is a tough teacher, but
a good one. Let God's love flow
through you to help those
who are hurting, needing the
love you can release to them.

Love is ...

It [love] always protects, always trusts,
always hopes, always perseveres.
~ 1 Corinthians 13:7 ~

Love is ...
Slow to suspect ... quick to trust.
Slow to condemn ... quick to justify.
Slow to offend ... quick to defend.
Slow to belittle ... quick to appreciate.
Slow to demand ... quick to give.
Slow to provoke ... quick to conciliate.
Slow to hinder ... quick to help.
Slow to resent ... quick to forgive.

Love in action

And now these three things remain: faith, hope and love. But the greatest of these is love.
~ *1 Corinthians 13:13* ~

Love's ABC's
Love Accepts, Behaves, Cheers, Defends, Enriches, Forgives, Grows and Helps. Love Includes, Joins, Kneels, Listens, Motivates, Notices, Overlooks, and Provides. Love Quiets, Respects, Surprises, Tries, Understands, Volunteers, Warms, Expects, and Yields. Love in action breaks the code that adds Zip to your life!

Willing and open

"I am the Lord's
servant," Mary answered.
~ Luke 1:38 ~

God's love is expressed through
other people to us. You don't have
to be a perfect saint to be able to
share love with someone else. You
don't even have to be especially mature
as a Christian to share God's love.
You just have to be willing and open.

Give your broken heart to God

*Surely he took up our infirmities
and carried our sorrows ... and
by his wounds we are healed.*
~ Isaiah 53:4-5 ~

God can heal your heart. God
can rescue you from despair
and give you something to rejoice
about again. It won't happen
overnight, but it will happen.
All you have to do is be
willing to give every piece of
your broken heart to God.

The gift of God's love

"You are the light of the world.
A city on a hill cannot be hidden."
~ Matthew 5:14 ~

Give every single little piece
of your heart to the Lord, and
He will begin the mending
process. You will survive,
times will get better, and you
will, with the grace of
God, be able to help others
with the gift of God's love.

Some love homework

Let no debt remain outstanding,
except the continuing debt to love
one another, for he who loves his
fellowman has fulfilled the law.
~ Romans 13:8 ~

Give yourself some love homework
this month. Assign yourself the task
of loving someone you don't really
like. I don't mean that you will make
yourself her best friend, but determine
(make a decision of the will) that you
will be obedient to Christ
and love her, in spite of
her shortcomings. God
will bless you for that.

You are going to make it

*May the God of hope fill you with
all joy and peace as you trust in him,
so that you may overflow with hope
by the power of the Holy Spirit.*
~ Romans 15:13 ~

After the storm is over, there are
bittersweet memories. After the first few
months of shock and panic, some of the
pain is drained off and healing begins. You
begin to feel better for longer periods of
time. You can go for a few hours and not be
consumed by thoughts of your
wayward child. Then, pretty
soon, you can survive a
whole day without anguish.
That is when you know you
are going to make it after all!

42

Love invested

" ... weep for ... your children. For
the time will come when you will
say, 'Blessed are the barren women,
the wombs that never bore and
the breasts that never nursed!'"
~ Luke 23:28-29 ~

What we mothers have to
recognize is that it is all right to
hurt – hurt is a measure of the
love we have invested in someone
else. There is risk involved with love,
and too often, heartache. But the
alternative is a life of gray
and dullness.

That kind of love

*Having loved his own who
were in the world, he now showed
them the full extent of his love.*
~ John 13:1 ~

The love of a parent for a child
should be a reflection of the
love God has for each of his
spiritual children. That's a love
that can be hurt. That's a love
that can cause pain. That's a
love that can suffer, but can't be turned
off. That kind of love is precious.

Sharing our hurt

*"My command is this: Love each
other as I have loved you. Greater
love has no one than this, that he lay
down his life for his friends."*
~ John 15:12-13 ~

Finding a refuge ... isn't that what
we are all doing? People who hurt
as we hurt need a place to cry, a
person to care, the security of intimate
friends who will share our hurt.

A refuge for someone else

*... make every effort to add to
your faith ... godliness; and to
godliness, brotherly kindness,
and to brotherly kindness, love.*
~ 2 Peter 1:5 7 ~

Sometimes the Lord directs us to
become places of shelter and
hope for others. Have you ever
thought about being a refuge for
someone else? Few roles are more
gratifying, but in
order to be a refuge
for someone else, you
need to be loving,
compassionate, and accepting.
Christians, we need each other!

Together

As iron sharpens iron, so
one man sharpens another.
~ Proverbs 27:17 ~

You can begin your own healing
by being a refuge for someone
else. You can do for others
what you need for yourself.
Open your heart to someone
else, even when you are in
pain yourself. Together you
can encourage each other
and pray for each other.

Today is here

Whatever your hand finds to do, do it
with all your might, for in the grave, where
you are going, there is neither working
nor planning nor knowledge nor wisdom.
~ Ecclesiastes 9:10 ~

Dream not too much of
what you'll do tomorrow,
how well you'll work another
year; tomorrow's chance
you do not need to borrow –
today is here.